W9-DCF-257

# OUL REFLECTIONS

PERSONAL ODYSSEY IN POETRY AND PAINTINGS

*by*

MIRIAM JASKIEROWICZ ARMAN

BN NUMBER  0-9674181-2-7

inted In The United States of America
ɔvember 2002

All paintings featured in the book are available on beautiful 8 x 10
Ceramic tiles in a limited edition.

For information please contact:

Music Visions International, PO Box 17345 Plantation, FL 33317

or by email: musicvisions@aol.com

# *DEDICATION*

To You, Aviva, my beloved daughter, my beautiful spirit, r inspiration, I dedicate these poems and paintings as expression of my life. Your memory lives on in my writing my teaching, and my very essence as a human being. Yo legacy continues in every word, every thought...alwa and forever.

To you, my father Jonas Jaskierowicz: I cherish yo memory, Your Judaism, your teachings, your wisdom, yo integrity, and your truth.... Give that my life does yo honor.

To my ancestors, The Sages, To Six Million who perishe my guides, my tradition, my people, whose history ar tragedies have shaped who I am. Ani Maamin! .... I believe

Mother and Child                                    Pastel On Paper

Soul Reflections

# My Gift

### Thank You to the Rebbe

Enlightment is Offered to One Who Seeks:
A beginning, An end, A future - Today!
Forever Unaware on the Conscious Plane-
Knowledge to be felt, Yours and Mine -
Now!

Conceive your Own Perfection!
Accept Wholeness, Totally Experience Infinity -
Universe, Yours is the Essence of Self.

The Light returns me Home - I am Welcome!
Choices have Indicatd My Journey -
Fast, furious Events, Reeling Emotions,
Intellect facing dark Nights of the Soul -
Illuminate my Perceptions...
An Opening;

The Path Demands My Waiting, Yearning -
Hope endlessly speeds the Celebration of Life.
My Beingness moves through the process,
Ignites Flames, Validates the Journey,
The fervent Quest, My Life!
Existence.

Forgive Judgements, Foibles, Faithlessness-
Free me! At last to Be - To Fly -
To Soar, Be One.. Be Me

# Eyes - Soul Speak

There, a Moment in Silence,
All Ceases - Nothing Exists -
Stillness, Absolute and Total:
I Enter,
Finding Darkness and Light,
Emptiness and Completion -
Paradox!

In That Place, Clarity, Understanding...
Essence of Spirit - Truth -
Divine Love.

My Being Pulsates with Stillness,
Pure Energy of Knowing...
Consciousness!

In Barrenness... Volume,
In Space, Essence and Growth Exists!

Here My Core Lives-
Illuminated;
Drinking from the Well,
Nourishing Sweet Waters of an Earth,
Blessed with Fruit -
Milk and Honey -
Seeing with Eyes that Search Beyond;
Finding the Realm of Knowing -
Without Question nor Explaination...

Here Reigns the Absolute -
Tone!
Finding Perfect Expression -
Sound!
In Nothingness, My Soul Quenches its Thirst -
Replenished, Refreshed, Strengthened -
Singing!
Ready for Life - Once More.

Soul Reflections

# EXPRESSIONS OF MY LIFE

Come With Me On A Voyage Into The Vast Abyss
Of The Human Soul And Witness The Transformation Of
My Feelings Into Color, Form And Verbal Images. The
Exteriors Are Stripped Away And Only The Essence
Remains.... Feel My Work - Not As I Do - But Exorcise Your
Own Demons And Find Peace...Look Into My Soul And
See The Depths Of Despair, Experience The Deepest
Love, Caring, Joy And Happiness...My Passions!

★

Explore The Psyche Of Each And Every Image...Interpret
My Life, Because Each Piece Represents The Sum Total
Of My Being...
I Hold Back Nothing...I Give It All To YOU...
Judge It, Fear It, Adore It, But Most Of All – Feel It!

★

Since Childhood, Poetry Has Been A Way For Me To
Express My Deepest Self ...Few People Ever Knew That.
Few Know Me - My Thoughts, My Dreams,
My Joys And My Pains, My Loves. In My Poems
I Can Cry, While On The Outside, I Remain In Control.
In My Poems, As Well My Paintings, I Strip Away The
Pretense Of Life And Let Go Of My Emotions, My
Desires, My Fears...I Allow Myself To Touch My Soul, My
Heart, My Being.

So Great Has Been My Loss, That I Thought I
Would Not Find The Words To Express My Self In Poem
Yet When I Wrote "My Flower," My Beautiful Daughter
Aviva Came To Life And With Her Gentle Inspiration And
Guidance, I Found The Strength To Share My Poetry, My
Feelings About So Many Things, With You. She Made Me
Promise Two Things Before She Left Me: "Write And Pain
- The World Needs To Know You".
I Promised And I Fulfill My Promise Here And Now.

The More I Live, The More I Understand That There Is
Nothing In Life More Important Than To Be Totally And
Completely Honest With Oneself And Everyone You Come
Contact With; That It Is Hardly Important What Someone
Thinks Of Your Ideas, Your Feelings, You...
The Greatest Thing You Can Do In Life, Is To Give Of
Yourself. I Do That Every Day In My Teaching, With My
Students, My Friends –
Here I Am Giving You All Of Me,
No Holding Back, No Escaping.
It Is My Fervent Hope That In My Words You Find
Expressions Of Your Own Life And That Through My
Humble Attempt At Giving To You, You In Turn Share
Yourself With Those In Your Life.

Soul Reflections

When I Have An Exhibition And See My Works On
The Walls Of The Gallery, I Am Fully Exposed, Revealed,
Naked. Everything I Am, Everything I Will Ever Be, Past,
Present And Future, Is There For All To See. There Is No
Shame, No Blame, No Uncertainty, And No Regret...
I Exist To Share My Heart And Myself With You.

★

All Of What You See And Read, Makes Up " Me" - The
Woman, The Artist, The Poetess, The Human Being. This
Is How I Perceive The World Around Me.
You May Love My Work, You May Hate It -
Please, Just Don't Be Indifferent --
React! That Is Most Important And Crucial...
You Have Not Passed Me Over
And For This I Thank You.

*Miriam Jaskierowicz Arman*

# TABLE OF CONTENTS

Soul Reflections

# A Million Miles

Another Life, Another Time...
Through The Tunnel
...In, To Live
...Out To Die
I Have Come A Million Miles
From Other Realms, From Other Spheres;
To Try  Again.... Once More...
To Find Completion...

Help Me, Guide Me, Love Me, Trust Me, Feel Me,
Let Me Be Me.......
I Beg You!

I Remember The Tunnel, The Bright Lights
The Souls I Knew And Loved
Who Sent Me On My Way...
To This Life Time,
Who Cautioned...
Beware Beloved, Beware This Time....
To Live Correction...
I Carry With Me Birthright,
The Last Time....

Past Knowledge Of Lifetimes Spent
In Flight, In Deserts, In Forests, Villages,
Many Lands, Different Times;
Held, Loved, Powerfully Pursued,
Spent, Crying, Sighing, Wounded, Wailing,
Suffering, Burning, Screaming, Escaping...
Suffocating In The Dregs Of Blood.

I Look To Remember, To Feel, To Understand
Where I Have Been, What I Have Done...
How I Have To Be, What I Have To Know....

I Feel The Burn Of The Ages  Upon  My Breast.
Branded Crest Of The Fathers....
The Blood Of Sages Running Through My Veins,
Reminding Me..... You Are ... We Are ... They Are....
Universe Large And Small...
Still And Booming
Hear My Cry, My Pleading,
My Raging, My Furor, Delirium, Frenzy, My Ranting...

Save And Preserve The Child!

Don't Let It Slide Into The Abyss
Only To Be Lost Again....
Quench This Painful Need ...
The Fire Inside-
To Be Whole ...To Be Sane —
Open Mind ... Heart, Soul ... To Comprehend....
Experience, Savor, Taste, Feel,
This Life Time...
Not To Have Lived Again Without Attainment....

Soul Reflections

# Above The Horizons

Stay, My Light,
Don't Go Away:
Believe, I Will Be By Your Side
To  Cherish This Life...
The One I Created For  You,
For Me,
With You,
For  Us.

Come, Walk The Glistening Shores,
Breathe Life In Turquoise Gulps
Of  Endless Worlds Below.
Take My Hand,
Don't Let Go,
Lest I Fly Alone, Carried, Like A Bird
Into Yonder,
Above The Horizons,
Beyond Your Reach
No Beginning- No End.

Spirit Lives Here,
But Alone,
Without A Guide,  Just To Be.

Have I Told You How I Miss You?
Have I Touched Your Mind Tenderly?
Filled You With My Aroma?
Do You Long To Fly With Me,
Into Spaces, Where You And I Are One?

Fly Then, My Love,
On My Angels Wings
For Truth Loves Company,
And We Are Love.

Voodu                                                    Mixed Media

*Soul Reflections*

# Autumn

Giant Footsteps Of My Life-
Where Do You Lead Me So Soon!

From Reckless Youth, Abandon, Frolic:
To The Autumn Of My Days-
Thinking Foolishly I Would Live Forever.

Tattered Is My Heart To Know,
That You Exist Only Behind The Veil-
Me, Reaching Through The Clouds,
To Touch You One More Time,
Just Once.
Tell You Things, I Never Said.
Pity!
Where Is ME, Where Have I Gone?
Have You Forgotten The Child,
The Senseless, Hopeful Child Inside?
Joyful, Always Smiling, Idealistic...
Where Is SHE?

Lost World That Cannot See,
Will Not Hear Confessions,
Ranting Despair.

Look Deep Within The Heart Of Mankind;
Follow Me Into The Abyss Of My Being...

Am I So Transmuted,

So Jaded,

So Afraid,
To NOT Believe In Life Or Love?

# Break Through

Life Revives Sparkles, Glimmers,
Surges Of Power And Strength,

Eyes Bright;
Electricity, Powerfully Illuminating:

Potent!
Alive, Resting,
Flow And Resisting,
Desperately Torn Apart, Yet Together,
Flying High, Yet Ground Bound : Searching!
Remind Me Why I Am Here?

Reasons For My Existence?
Are There?
Measuring, Alluring, Remote, Resilient,
Innovative, Alive And Surviving.
Everyday Anew, Resolving To Be,
To Stay, To Exist

A Path Beyond The Day...
Reviving Bones From Dust And Ashes
Sent From Heaven To Earth Grave To Life.
Choices Constant, Never Ending Cycle:
Regeneration!

Brilliant Beams Of Light,
Flow Through The Center Of My Universe
Light Up My Life, Complete My Yearning....
Breath Of Life,

Culminating Spirit—
Music—

Song—

Balance In All Things.

Soul Reflections

Can Can                                        Pastel On Paper

# Dancing With The Wind

Look, The Leaves Are Dancing
To The Melody Of Humming Birds;
See How They Soar Into The Sky
And Slowly,
Ever So Softly
Whirl Onto The Ground...Finding Their Peace...
Would That It Be Me!

The Rain Gently Cools The Ground,
Fills The Soil With Life,
Nourishes Its Force;
Providing Endlessly, Giving, Sharing,
To You And Me....

Breathe In The Cool Night Air
And Feel The Tingles In Your Heart.
Touch The Sky With Your Finger Tips –

Find Wonder In A Word,
Realize The Totality Of The Universe
That Speaks Of Truth And Honesty
Integrity And Loyalty
The  Bed Rock Of Eternity.

Experience The Glow,
The Moment Of Understanding And Joy -
Speaking To G-D And Saying:
Let Me Be Deserving Of That Heart,
That Soul,
That Grace,
That Touch,

Please Make It Be Real....

Soul Of My Soul!

The Rabbi Valodia                                           Oil Pastel On Board

# Evacuation

Raids , Resettlements, Confusion,
Animal Stench Of Humanity ,
Cattle Cars - Beatings, Rape...
Harrowing Cries,
Tortured Wails
Relentlessly Piercing The Still Of Night.
My Child?
A Coat, It's Cold.
Where Are We Going?
Imploring: Don't Take Her!
My Child, Where Is My Child?

A Sea Of Bodies, Empty Faces,
Battered Humans, Desperation
Tortured Souls;
An Enemy Who Laughs And Sneers
Relishing The Pain And Sorrow Of His Captors.

They Took My Husband, My Sister-
Hallucinating In Her Pain,
She Screams...
Where Is My Sister, My Sister?

I Saw A Black Crow Pecking At My Window
Black Messenger Of Doom
My Tears Are Dry,
I Have No More...
I Beg You G-D,
Rachmunes, Have Pity!
Where Do I Go?
Where Do I Search?
Survival? Why? I Am Alone!
My Loved Ones Ripped From My Breast
Let Me Die....
Shame  Of My Existence.

Blackness Surrounds Me,
Despair Is My Companion.
A Shadow, Illusion, A Vision
My Wife
Her Smile, So Sweet, So Loved
Her Eyes Dulled, Lightless...
Death
And There, Our Daughter
Innocent, Smiling
Only Thirteen, A Blossom-
Gone,
Gone!

Soul Reflections

The words of this Poem and the Poem "Have Mercy" are dedicated to my mother Mila Jaskierowicz and are inspired by her poems. Her experiences in the concentration camps and the experiences of millions who did not survive, burn on my heart and have, to a great degree, shaped who I am.

May their plight and sacrifice never be forgotten and may we, who follow after them remember, that each of us has a responsibility to our fellow man, the key to our humanity. May we have learned never to allow the world to close its eyes again to the plight of peoples who suffer, no matter what their color, no matter their creed.

# Familiar Roads

Wandering Mind And Spirit...
Ever, Never, Forever - Restless.
Today Is Still Only Today...
Silver Skies, Floating Waves-
Motion...
Remind Me When I Was Flying With You
Amongst The Stratum -
So Close To You Always,
I Feel Your Nearness... Caught Adrift,
Between Reality And Illusion -
Separated By A Veil Of Clouds,
Searching For A Meaning To My Existence;
Understanding, That It Is You, Only You
Fulfilling My Destiny...

Existing, But For A Thread Of Truth,
In A Malignant And Static World -
Moving Through Dreams And Lies,
In A Blissful State Of Ignorance.
Here But For The Grace Of Light,
Do I Find My Way In The Darkness —
Familiar Roads Traveled,
Forever Unknown!

Hold Me                                    Oil Pastel On Paper

# For Love ~ A New Day

Evoke Thoughts, Dreams
Of Past Tears Cried,
Joys Found,
Growth, Healing, Blessings ~
Spiritual Openings
All In My Mind...
Body And Soul,
One:
Let Feelings Unfold.

Alone, I Stand, Naked,
A Grown Woman Child
In The Mirror of My Existence,
Looking And Finding
A Link Missing.

Tears creep into my eyes
Falling like raindrops
Replenishing My Soul.

I Thought Of You-
On The Beach,
Under The Stars,
In My Arms,
Touching,
Feeling, Sharing,
A Toast,
A Smile Shared,
Eyes Meeting,
Sacred Words Spoken....
Peace, Harmony,
Hopes And Dreams –
We Find Each Other,
We Belong –
Again!

Soul Reflections

# Maui Downhill

Taken To The Clouds,
Crossed Space,
Between Reality And Fantasy.
Volcanic Lava Stones;
Beware The Curse!

Flora Growing Low,
Hugging Mother Earth's Bosom.
Air, Crisp, Thin,
Breath Stops,
Close To G-D - Sensing His Presence;
Staring Into The Crater -
Grave Of A Million Years.

Spirits Live Here -
Voices Speak Silently,
Needing To Be Heard, Yet Not Seen.
Truth Of Ages,
Creep Beneath My Skin
Tantalizing, Tingling,
Lend Expression.
Are You Listening?

Do You Hear Me?
I Am Here To Protect You…
Grow, Choose Life, He Said!
Go If You Must…
Ride Safe….
Let The Wind Caress, Penetrate:
Burned Skin, Fortify, Satisfy -
Thrill To The Bone,
Replenish!
Feel Alive - Now…
Remember?
Rain, Clouds Open, Dark, Ominous…
Fear, Blind,
A Fall…Pain, Failure!
NO!
Take Courage, Persevere!
Elated Heart, Frolic, I Can, I Will Accomplish!
A Moment In Time, Deep Thought,
Clarity -
Remember?
Our Grace Chose You To Be,
Experience, Survive,
Dare The Fates…Beware!
Be Grateful For Life.Cherish-
Be, Once Again
The Victor.

Soul Reflections

# Listen To The Voice

Inspired by conversations with Reb Osher

Words Flow From His Lips. I Sense Them!
Silence Engulfs...Breath Halts - He Speaks .
The World Listens To The Sound Of A Voice,
Uttering Eternal Truth -

Blessings! Lend Your Ear!

We Have A Mission, You Said, A Destiny.
To Heal, To Help, To Teach - Be Whole!
Exemplify Humanity In Images, Actions, Deeds -
Painting Pictures Through Expressions -
Ancient Knowledge,
Nourishing, Enlightening:

Language Of The Soul...

Do You Understand My Plight? Help Me Then!

Follow!

Have You Heard Thoughts Pour From Me,
Connecting Memories, Generations, Universe,

You - Me

Far beyound our meager understanding ~

Reveal your Secrets.
Rise above your psyche, be clever, and be wise...

Behold the wisdom of sages encompass your being ~
Bathe in healing waters of the holy well,
Cleansing your weariness, your pain ~

Eternal Wanderer, Rest!
Dream, behold your inner voice, guide me; I beg
Instruct ethereal flow ~ Find Meaning in your Life

# Reborn in Love

My Strength Will Come In Dreams!
I Search, Believe, I Trust,
You Said: Good Bye My Love,
Don't Give Me Up!
Open The Door,
Enter The Dark,
Find Me.
Tenderness, Your Eyes, The Fire;
Your Tears Allure...
Think Only Of ME, My Love!


To The Sea -
Explore it's Viscous Power-
Damned Be Those Who Voyage Beyond Death!
Let Rebirth Be Choice-
Not Only Perception-


Loosing My Mind?
No, No, Never....
Don't Dare Give Up-
Groping, Snarling,
Grasping At Life In Deaths Throws...
Go Beyond -
Don't Drown My Life, I Beg You.

I Dig At My Soul ~
Accept Me.
I beg You!
Battered Soul Of My Sacrifice.

Gateway To Hell~
I Won't Give Up~
For Love Alone!
Look At Me~
Fire Surrounds, Death Survives~
Scared To Wake The Morning....
You In My Arms ~ Eternally

Dry My Tears

Pastel and Ink On Paper

*Soul Reflections*

# My Flower

In My Heart You Are A Tiny Rose,
Small And Delicate, Ever Beautiful,
Perfectly Bending In The Breezes
Of The Cool Spring Air.
Your Sweet Aroma Fills The Space,
Like Soft Caresses, Touching My Minds Eye.
Spring, My Darling, Ended To Soon.
You Spoke To Me Softly,   Always-
Every Word Imprinted On My Memory.
Your Smile Encompasses Me,
Like Balmy Waters Under Blue, Unending Skies.
Your Eyes Sparkling,  Always With Love.
I Feel You So Close- I Reach For You,
Behind The Veil Of Eternity
You Touch Me Gently, Whispering:
" Mommy, I Love You!"
My Tears Nourish Your Ground,
My Love Grows Your Memory,
My Purpose Gives You Unending Life!
Your Life - My Life- Never Apart

\*\*\*

*Dedicated To The Memory Of My Beautiful Daughter*
*AVIVA, Whose Life Is My Inspiration!*

# Only Butterflies Are Free

Light, Life And Being -
All Cramped Into A Moment In Time.
Seeing And Feeling, Holding And Touching
All Molded Into A Web Spun Of Thoughts And Tears,
Fleeing The Forests Of Darkness
Into The Brightness Of Day.

Sleep Eludes The Traveler -
Powerful Reference To Deserts Once Crossed,
Buried Deeply In Her Mind.
Parched Lips, Aching Limbs, Forever Searching
Never Finding
The Burning Bush, The Word, The Touch.
Passionate Desire -
Fires Blurring My Vision
I, Who Stare Into Nothingness To Find My Truth.

Satiate My Thirst At The Well  , Deep And Profound
Accept The Breath Of Life
Within The Budding Of Early Morning Light...
Fill My River Of Hope With New Experience!

Soul Reflections

Let Me Lie In His Arms
Relishing The Rays Of Early Morning Dawn...

Stretch Out Your Hand And Bask
In The Afterglow Of Passion;
Enchant The Universe With Your Smile.
Softly Caressing My Heart-
For Don't You See:

Only You And I And Butterflies Are Free!

# <u>Reflections</u>

There Are Moments In Life
When You First Discover Yourself...
When You Become Aware Of All You Are,
All You Want To Be,
Who You Can Be,
Where You Belong.

That Very Moment You Realize,
That Everything Which Was ,
Is Just A Piece In The Puzzle
Of  What Your Life Means Today-
And That Every Instant Past,
Is In Essence, Who You Are.

You Recall The Cruel Blows,
The Tearful Joys,
The Pain And Sorrows,
You Become Aware Of Inner Sounds  -
The Past,
Of Creating Your Future In The Present
Of Finally Being : Your Noblest Thought.

<u>Soul Reflections</u>

Warmth, A Glow, Completion
Awareness Enlightened-
The Total Meaning Of Life Begins To Take Form.


Your Dreams Reflect Your Desires,
Your Hopes And Cravings,
You Tune Into Your Heart,
You Experience Every Beat....
And Ultimately Understand Your Destiny.


Resolve Today:
To Be The Best You Can Be,
True Only To Yourself!
DARE!


Allow Pure Light To Guide You.
Trust Your Highest Instincts!
Do What Your Heart Tells You.
Feel Yourself Come Alive!
Breathe The Freedom Of Your Existence!
Be Whole,
Complete,
Be You.

# Music of My Heart

Energy, Life Giving, Sounds That Delight-
Voices That Fill My Mind With Gladness,
Butterflies Sensually Dancing,
To The Rustling Of Falling Leaves,
Tones That Nurture My Soul,
Notes That Delight My Senses,
Flowers That Sing Their Tunes;
Trees That Whisper Their Melodies
In Winds That Flow With The Universe...
Endlessly, Bellowing Drums, Day And Night.
Birds Chirping, Willows Murmuring.

The Music Of My Heart.
Beats To The Rhythm Of My Passion,
Revealed, Deeply Felt Expressions,
Secrets Spoken In Moments Of Love,
Cried In Pain, Expressed In Verses
Of Never Ending Tears-

Music, Fill My Being,
Tell Me Of The Light In My Soul-
Delight, Illuminate,

Send Me On My Way,
Accompany Today, Tomorrow And Always.

Soul Reflections

Self Portrait

Mixed Media On Paper

# Remembering A Dream

One Night, In Deep Slumber You Came To Me,
Gentle, Powerful, Smiling,
Full Of Life.
Embracing Me Softly  -
I Trembled.

You Spoke Of Times Past And Forgotten-
In Lives Remembered,
When You And I,
Lingering On Soft Meadows In Deep Forests,
Lay Gazing At The Sky,
Counting Stars.

You Looked So Tranquil Then,
So Loving
You Touched My Face, I Kissed Your Eyes,
Climbing Into The Depth Of My Being-
Holding Eternity - You And I.

Oh, How I Loved You Then-
Precious Memory.
Like Snowflakes Tumbling To The Ground,
Kissing The Earth, Nourishing, Illuminating
You Penetrated My Soul,
Wrapping Your Arms Around Me,
Holding, Feeling-
Revealed Secrets.

I Remember Now-The Flow, The Depth -
The Yearning - Gentle Torment,
Life Itself ;
I Miss You So….
Come To Me My Love!
I Pray,

Make My Dream Be Today.

# The Answer To My Quest

When I Think I Know The Answers,
I Realize That I Know Nothing.
When I Believe, I Found The Reason,
Something Makes Me Understand,
That All My Pretenses
Are But Feeble Gestures At Hiding My Truth.

Was There Ever A Time When I Allowed
The Reality, Of Who I Am,
What I Want,
Who I Want To Be,
Into The Soul I Aspire To Behold?

Is There A Moment In Time
When I Allow Myself To Be
Totally And Completely ME?

It Is Only Now, I Have Opened The Door
It Is Here, That I Create My Being
It Is Today That I Vow:
To Let, To Receive, To Behold, To Encompass,
To Marvel, To Give, To Share, To Love
The Humanity That Is

" I "

# The Mirror

Look Into My Eyes And See My Soul--
Behold Their Power!
Satiate Your Desire.
Drink Deeply From The Wells Of My Passion
Taste The Flower Of My Tears.
Creep Into The Depths Of My Dreams--
Envision The Shine Of Pools Of Green,
Reflecting The Depth Of A Limitless Universe.

Enter My World Of Fantasy And Color . . ..
Peer Into The Deepest Crevices Of My Being,
Unveiling Reality To Only Behold The Truth;
The Endlessness Of Miles Traveled--
The Past, The Present, The Future.

This Mirror Never Lies, Never Hides--
It Simply Reflects That Which Is,
Which Was--And Will Always Be.
So Take My Hand,
Don't Be Afraid.
Look Beyond The Heavens To The Stars . . ..
Feel, Touch, And Know-
Me!

EDITORS CHOICE AWARD - The International Library of Poetry. Library 2

Soul Reflections

# The Silent Killer - The Memories

You See A Stranger —

Old And Gray,
Withered Away, Remote And Senile.
He Sits Alone, Forgotten,

Lost Soul.
Life Bent His Limbs Too Soon...

Why?
Dulled Eyes - Echoes Of Yesterday-

Gone!
Pain Warped His Back-

He Seems To Sleep.
Your Heart Remembers The Young Man,
Full Of Glory In His Day, Boundless Energy
Proud To Stand, To Fight, To Live, To Love!
Who Is That Shadow Crouched On The Porch?
Remember, Papa, How We Laughed And Sang?
How Life Ran Away And I With It?
Forgive Me, I Beg You -

Where Is That Time?
Where Are Those Days Of Ease And Joy And  "Us "?
You Have Forgotten Me? Don't Know My Name?
Your Eyes Stare Blank. Look, Your Child Is Here!
My Heart Is Breaking, You Can't See!
Cruel Blow, No Memory, Oblivion...Blind!

If You Must Go, Then Take With You,
My Memory Of Loving You To All Eternity.

*Dedicated to the memory of Bernie Fox*

# Belonging

On the Way to Self Awareness 1976

When days Rush by,
Leaving just empty spaces in my mind,
I wish I belonged ~

When Black thoughts
Encompass the recesses of my troubled soul ~
I wish I belonged

When pain racks my body
And forces its way into my subconscious ~
I wish I belonged

But who would want to share such a sorry existence
Would you ??

Soul Reflections

# Unread Poems Of My Heart

I Feel The Smile, My Senses Light,
The Aroma Of Jasmine Seems Sweeter
Suddenly My Heart Beats Faster;
Moments To Cherish-

Time Stands Still.
Can You Feel My Longing
To Hear The Sound Of Your Voice,
See The Smile On Your Face?
Glistening Eyes- Kiss Your Tears Away,
Search Your Mind For Memories,
Of Old Hurts And Pain...
Hold You, Feel You,

Make You Whole!
It's Been Too Long Without You,
A Lifetime It Took To Find You,
To Share My Mind, To Find The Words —
Unread Poems Of My Heart:

Create Tomorrows, Forget Yesterdays Sorrows,
Journey Through The Years With Me,
On Petals Of Roses, Softness Of Clouds
And Be What Is Real, For Eternity.

# A Day Like No Other

It Was A Day Unlike Any Other
Though It Seemed To Anyone Else Quite Usual.
Late fall, Beautiful Sunshine,
Early Morning Hour
A Cry, A Smile,
A Birth
Then You!

Above It All,
A Gate
At The Beginning Of Time
A Word, A Gesture
The Promise Was Made In Heaven
When G-D Decided
To Send You,
A Soul From Long Ago,
On This Very Day A Drop Into Eternity.

You Remember Each Year
Each Tear, Each Joy,
Each Pain, Each Happy Hour,
Each Loving Moment,
Each Torment, You Recall In This Lifetime.

Soul Reflections

Do You Remember The Other Times?
Long Ago, In Other Lives:
Holding Hands, Racing Through Meadows-

You Were Always So Strong,
So Powerful, So Loving,
Always There, Always Mingling Into My Thoughts.
So Here You Are Again
On Such A Special Day Far Away,
Yet In My Thoughts Sending You A Star
To Guide You This And Every Year
Throughout This Lifetime,
Into Eternity.

I Send You Love And Warmth,
Feelings And Joy,
A Rose For Fragrance Of Me,
A Soft Kiss To Mellow You.

# Behold The Box

Follow The Vistas Of My Passion-
Rush To The Fields Of My Dreams -
Hallowed Roses I Plant, From Seeds Of Old.

Take From Me The Light.
Give Without Fright Or Misgivings,
Share The Wonders Of The Universe,
Without Demand Or Care -
Take Your Questions And Prayers,
Pain And Sorrow, Your Thoughts And Desperation -
Put Them In The Box ...
Close Up Tight, Red Ribbons To Tie -
Behold - Freedom!!

Take The Sky Of Blue, Rain,
Clouds, Fields And Mountains,
The Forests-And Take Then You-
You,
The Essence Of All Humanity
The Life Force And Burning Desire
Conquer!
Join The Earth's Lifeblood,
The Good, The Strong - Destinal Resolve -
And Demand Your Right "To Be"

Soul Reflections

We                                                    Mixed Media On Canvas

# An Image Of My Love

I Dreamt Of You Tonight;
I Sigh, Allow Myself To Feel.
With You, My Love,  Eternally.

In Emerald Pools Of Endless Depth,
I See Your Passion, Your Fire -
Reflections Of Dawns In Still Lagoons,
Burning Desire, Tender Touch,
In Star Filled Nights,
Lying Still, Embracing,
Lost In The Music Of Night Time Rhapsodies.

Come To Me Beloved!
Share With Me The Moment,
Caress, Tenderness And Peace-
In Bliss Under Moonlit Skies,
A Silhouette, A Smile, A Kiss -
Holding, Touching, Being-
No More Restraint, We Have The Right,
To Love Without Regret,
Expression of Life Itself,

NOW!

# An Invitation

Have I Told You Where I Am Going?
Come Along, Share My Excitement.
Flying On The Wings Of Eagles,
Into The Blue Yonder Of Tomorrow.
Did I Mention Lakes And Forests,
I Wanted To Explore
Roads Un-Traveled;
Tall Mountains, I Wanted To Climb?

Did I Tell You Of The Wilderness,
The Deserts, The Oceans,
The Streams That Call And Beckon Me,
To Ride The Waves, Search Beneath The Sea
For Treasures Untold, Yet To Behold?
Come With Me To Lands Uncharted-
You And I, Adventuring Together,
Savoring Precious Moments-
Pleasure, Desire-
Harmonizing Sounds Filling Space,
Delighting, Tantalizing Our Senses.
Come Lead The Way To Endless Laughter...
Warming Sunshine, Sparkling Raindrops,
To Keep, To Hold These Memories,
Always

Soul Reflections

# Of Dreams Will Come

A Soul Never Quite Known,
A Life, Never Quite lived....
A Beauty Never Bloomed In Full -
In My Minds Eye,
I Behold The Person You Will Never Be.

In The Valley Of The Souls,
I Search To Bring You Back...
Journey Through Fire,
Illuminated By Love
And The Power Of My Dreams.

Thoughts,
Pure Color; That Scent Of Roses,
Silence And Strength For You-
For Us-
Choose Life, My Love!
Fly With Your Choices.
Sleep Precious One - Never Give Up!

Hell Will Swallow Your Soul -
But Reality Is Mine-
Your Direction?
Rebirth!

The Veil Of My Survival
Devastates My Senses,
Flower Of My Destiny –

Rainbow In The Depth Of Hades,
Illuminate My Soul!
Remind Me Whom I Love–
Don't Disappear... Ever!

\*\*\*

*Dedicated to the Memory of My Beautiful Daughte*
*Aviva*

Art Is Everything                              Mixed Media and Sculpture On Canvas

# Live Today

Passing Days,  One Into The Other-
Nothing Stops The Flow;

Lost Memories-
Burning Pain Of Loneliness-

Void-
Neither Touch Nor Smile,

Humanity Lost
Moments Measured In Time,

Encapsulated.
Shining Spirit Brimming With Love,
Oh Beauty Of Life -

Watchful Time Of Youth
Where Is The Magic?
Soaring,  Expanding,  Vast Horizons.
A Bird In Flight,  Searching,
The Limitless Expanse Of Sky And Clouds,
For One Lost,  So Long Ago,  Never Forgotten.

Was It The Depth Of His Glance?
The Incomparable Emotion When Kissed?
His Touch?

Truth Realized, Magical Openings.
Was It So?

Was It Real?

Do You Remember?

Today Is Here; The Night Has Passed-
New Vistas To Discover, Emotions To Feel -
Let Go Of The Past,

Live Today!

Live!
New Day Caress Me,

Make Love To Me.

\*\*\*

*Inspired By Robert Claude Feldman,
A True Musical Genius Of His Time*

*Thank You*

<u>Soul Reflections</u>

# Canvas Reflections

I Breathe It -
The World Is Fading Away
Color Exists, Shape, Form, Depth And Space-
I Relate To The Infinite -
Speak To Me In Abstract Terms,
So I Understand You.
Genius Created In Memories Of Soft Lines
And Psychotic Behaviors,
Endless Passion -
Surreal Realism Enrapture My Being,
Hold The Spell And Remind Me Of Who I Am.
I Fly On The Wings Of Bright Soft Color-
Dots, Lines, Circles, Ovals, Ecliptics-
Rhyme The Colors Of Infinity,
Webbings —
Into Shapes Of Violet, Rose Colored Fabric.
The Nude Reflects Her Lover's Touch
In The Sensual Curves Of Her Voluptuous Body,
Sliding On Flowered Spaces, Into Oblivion.
My Head Is Spinning Out Of Control
In The Aura Of A Decadent Past Of Luxuries.
Sacred Shrines, Hallowed Spaces In My Mind,
Drink Color, Digest Form -
Live Again!

# Have Mercy

Cold And Gray Is November.
Layers Of Frost Chill Our Roofs,
Hundreds Without Warmth,
Without Shelter Or Food,
Crying For Mercy And Bread.

Cruel Winter Approaches-
Prepare, But How?
No Help In Sight,
Just Tears And Endless Sorrow.
The Chill Of Death Upon Our Breast
We Are The Poor, Suffering And Dying.
Oh, That We Could Huddle Close
Warm Our Bodies,
Find Comfort
Replenish Our Desperate Souls...

There On The Roadside, A Vagabond,
Crouched, Forlorn And Tattered
Raising His Hand To G-D,
Lamenting, Moaning In Pain-
His Cries Piercing The Cold Night Air
Shma' Israel Hashem,
Do You Hear My Plea?
Have Mercy My G-D , Forsake Me Not...

_Soul Reflections_

And Then There Are Those Passing Him By,
Laughing Carelessly,
Their Bellies Full,
Wrapped In Their Furs,
Hands Tucked Into The Warmth Of A Muff

They Do Not Fear Winter, Nor  Cold
They Feel Not The  Piercing Pain Of Hunger
They Pay No Heed To The Poor,
The Forsaken;
Those  Barely Alive.
No One  Sees  Or Hears Them,
No One Cares If They Live Or  Die,
No One Listens To The Destitute.

They Are The True Believers!
Only G-D Will Hear Their Cries!
Ani Maamin. I Believe!

# Miracles Of Ages

Flying On The Wings Of Angels
I Hear Celestial Music
Floating On The Clouds Of Endless Horizons
I Feel The Eyes Of The Sages Upon Me-
They Search My Heart
For Eternal Understanding, For Love!
Have I Forgotten To Open My Mind?
Have I Shut My Eyes,
Not Looked To Find Their Truth?
Is It The Pain That Has Kept Me Closed...
Awaiting The Miracle Of Love
To Open My Center,
To All There Is And Ever Can Be?
Fly Thoughts,
Enter The Realm Of Universal Light,
Sing The Songs Of My Existence
Release My Fears,
Permeate My Spirit,
Allow Me Peace!
Cleanse My Heart From Sorrow;
Empty My Vessel
Fill Me - Make Me Whole Again....
Soul Of My Soul,
Enlighten, Nourish, Illuminate,
I Beg You..............

Soul Reflections

# The Birthday

Like The Sun Upon The World,
Strong Stands The Tree Of Your Existence,
Rooted Deeply Into The Folds Of Earth's Bosom-
Warming, Soothing, Nurturing Endlessly-
Replenishing Your Spirit, Your Soul,
Illuminating Your Life!
Trust In The Process,  For It Is Good!
Examine The Furrows Of Your Brow -
Smile At Lessons Learned,
Tears Shed With Grace And Knowing -The Pains -
Your Past Is Experience You Have Earned,
Your Future, The Fruits Of Your Labor.
Days Pass Like Shadows,
One Into The Other,  Relentlessly.
Arise Life  Force !  Uplift The Trunk -
Revive Youth's Fervor And Zest!
Out  Of The Ashes Of The Past   Grows Love
Strengthened And Empowered By Destinal Resolve.
Look Forward To Tomorrow,
Embrace The Joys Yet To Unfold.
Turn Your Branches To The Sky-
Allow 'Hashem' To Kiss Your Eyes,
Creating Sweetness And Harmony
In The Composed  Music Of Your New Tomorrows.

# Bathing In Moonlight

Save The Words-
Flow Now, Give To Me... Endlessly.
Join The Resonance's Of Sounds,
That Speak Words Of Love...

Bind The Flowers Of Patience
Into A Wreath Of Understanding -
Secrets Spoken,
Moments Of Passion Released,
Caresses, Blessed By Peaceful Demands -
Looks Full Of Passion,
Unspoken Words Of Love,
Recognized,  A Pair Of Eyes,
Slaves -
Gaze And Smile, Show My Feelings...
Look At Me This Way-
I Want You Now!
Drink From The Sunlight,
Steal Precious Moments...

Soul Reflections

Moon Light I Bathe In,
Held Feelings,
Closing Every Door.
Brake My Silence-
I Need You To Touch Me.
Curtains Drawn, To Welcome The Dawn-
Heal With Light.
I Caress You Softly,
Drink Your Dreams With Kisses,
Forever And Always Imprinted On My Mind.

# A Lifetime

We Strive For Possessions!
Confident We Own Time -
Yet, Owned By Time, We Are!
We Search For Love,
Speeding Through Life,
Endlessly Desiring, Never Satisfied-
Chances Lost,
Precious Moments Squandered
Thinking We Are Masters,
Arrogant And Superficial . . .
We Remain Alone -
Humanity Lost!
Acquiring Wealth, Amassing Fortune-
Greed . . ..
Stop!

Savor The Breeze....
Spring Passes Too Fast . . .
Eternity Commands! Destiny Rules!
So Live, Love, Give, Share, Strive For Goodness!
Your Life Is Sweet Music

Sing It!

Soul Reflections

Sabbath Candles

Three Dimensional Glass Fusion On Gla

*Soul Reflections*

# Shabbat Shalom

When Shabbat Descends
And The Sun Goes Down,
The Week Comes To An End ....
Slowly The Spirit Of Holiness
Illuminates The Sky
Opening Our Hearts With Festive Thoughts.

Light The Candles, Rekindle Hope,
Say The Words And Pray For G-D's Guidance.
Feel The Wistful Warmth Of Light
And Come To Terms With Seven Days Past.

A Time To Renew.
A Time To Regenerate—
A New Week;
Filled With Possibilities And Adventure.

Resolve To Be The Best You Can Be,
Joyfully Declare The Intentions Of Your Future,
Observe The Flame, As It Bends To Your Thoughts
And Rises To The Heavens,
Opening Doors To Your Prayers.

Accept The Blessings,
Open To The Light
Rejuvenate Your Thoughts
And Find Your Faith.
When Shabbat Descends
Put Aside The Woes Of Yesterday,
Evoke A Bright Tomorrow.

Baruch Ata Adoshem, Eloheinu Melech Ha Olam
Asher Kidischano Bemitzvotav Vezivanu, Lehadlik Nei
Shel Shabbat.....
Amen

*Soul Reflections*

# Please Live

Why my friend, do you want to die?
Extinguish not your light, I plead ...

My words fall like tears on desert stone,
Barren soil, Salty, Lifeless pillars,
Empty vessels without meaning....

You question your existence?
So do I - You question love and honor,
So do I - Human prerogative...foibles....

Life is senseless, worthless, useless, you said;
Pained, anguished....You are not alone....
You have lost too many times,
Cried to unanswering G-d's -
Searched For a reason to exit....

Death is good you say, easy....Sleep...Relief...
I understand. I too have shared your wanderings-
Yearning for safety, dreams, truth...
Disappointed, discouraged, lost...alone...
Crushed, shattered...I survived...rebuilt...again!

Accept! Here, take my hand,
Deny not my offering, I beg...
Lets walk the fields, Drink from the well,
Nourish our souls, Search out the clouds,
Bathe in the rain, Laugh again,
Do it for me....For I love thee!

Some Weeks Shortly Before The Publication Of This Book, I Was In New York, Teaching.

I Had Not Been At The Metropolitan Museum Of Art For Quite A Number Of Years.... 20 Or More.... Something Kept Me Away...

No, Not Something...I Kept Myself Away – My Way Of Negating My Real Need For Painting, For Art, For Creating.

I "Create" A Great Deal For Others In My Teaching, But Since The Loss Of My Beautiful Daughter Aviva, Almost Six Years Ago, I Have Not Been Able To Paint, Even Though My Art Works Had Brought Me International Accolades And Critical Acclaim In The Past.

Why? Well, My Paintings Became Too Personal, Too Revealing, Too Open, Especially At A Time, When I Had Closed Up, Shut Down... I Was Certain, That By Avoiding The Museum, Which I Loved More Than Any Other In The World, I Would Certainly Accomplish My Goal...Seclusion,

Isolation, Denial.

The 'Sensible' ME Had Decided Not To Share Myself Anymore, Not To Allow Closeness.... To Protect Myself Against Hurt, Against The Outside World That Only Stole And Betrayed.

This Time, Quite Against My Will, Moved By Some Incredible Force, Unable To Resist, It Seemed, Through The Portals Into The Familiar, Unfamiliar Space, I was drawn....

I Was Another Person.... I Could Not Remember Who I Was The Last Time I Entered.... I Just Knew, That I Was Not Who I Am Today. Ultimately It Really Does Not Matter.

I Am Who I Am.

I Cannot Remember What I Thought, What I Felt . I Bought A Drawing Book And A Pen ... Some Part Of Me Began Writing, Began Drawing- Totally Separated From The Other- Finding Herself Again.The Automatic Writings Which Follow Are Unedited, Exactly The Way I Wrote

Them.

      After I Left The Museum, I Returned To My Hotel And Cried For Hours, Uncontrollably. At First I Could Not Understand Why .... Only Adding to My Total Confusion.

      Many Hours Later I Understood, That There Had Been An Opening. Something Had Happened To Me... Something Deeply Buried Inside Had Loosened, Released. Years Of Pain Unraveled, Hurts Surfaced That I Had Not Wanted To Address, Had Put Into My " Boxes". A Profound Shift Had Taken Place. My Heart Was Beating Again.... I Felt Free and Alive....
I Was Ready To Face And Accept A New Life, No- My New Life!

      After Re-reading The Writings, I Took Meaningful Phrases And Incorporated Them Into Poems Which You Have Read— So If They Sound Familiar— You Are Right...

# Automatic Writings

I Breathe It...The World Seems To Fade Away
Color Exists And Shape And Form And
Depth In Space...
I Relate To The Infinite - Speak To Me In Abstract
Terms, So I Will Understand You -

Genius Created In Memories Of Soft Lines
And Psychotic Behaviors, Surreal Realism --
Enrapture My Being, Hold The Spell And
Remind Me Of Who I Am.

Evoke In My Death Still Flowers, Who Live In Color
And Die In Browns And Greens...
Water Lilies: Depth Of Dreams Lost And
Made Into Rivers.

I Fly On The Wings Of Bright And Soft Color Dots
-- Lines And Circles, Ovals And
Ecliptics-

Rhyme The Colors Of Infinity Into The Shapes Of
Sensual Fabrics.

The Nude Reflects Her Lover's Touch In The
Sensual Curves Of Her Voluptuous Body -- Sliding
On Flowered Spaces Into Oblivion....

My Head Is Spinning In The Aura Of
Decadent Pasts And Luxuries; Overpowering
Feelings Of Lives Lived And Past,
Experienced In A World Of Images Blown Out
Of Proportion By Flurries Of Remembrances....

Sacred Shrines Of Hallowed Spaces In My
Mind, Soul Reflexes -
Sending Chills Down My Spine -
I Drink The Color, Digest The Form-
Elaborate On Controversies Beyond My
Understanding -
Sorrow Follows Me Like A Bird Traveling To Warmer
Vistas-
Expressions Of Truth...

Soul Reflections

I've Know I Am Alone, Yet For The First Time
In Years, I Feel Complete - Together -
Apart From My Own Being - Satisfied With It...
I Look At A Sea Of Faces - None Like Mine, Each
Different, Each Individual
Each Full Of Secrets And Each Beautiful
Onto Itself -

Brilliant Flow Of Light Through The Center
Of The Universe -
Light Up My Life And Complete My Yearning....
Breath Of Life -
Culminate In The Spirit Of Music -
The Song, Laughter And Tears -
Balance In All Things............
Is There Truth? Is There Love? Is There Freedom? Is
There Life, Or Is It Just An Illusion,
All A Virtual Reality Of Nothingness In Space?
Like, Who Am I? Am I Real. Do I Fit?....
Or Am I A Misfit Onto Others And Myself?
Is It Real ?--
Look At Him-He Smiles. Does He Or Is He Frowning
-- Showing Me His Teeth??? -

The Sun Remembers To Shine -- The Moon
Remembers To Glow And I Fly Into The Realm
Of Illusion On The Wings Of A Butterfly...

Rest Weary Mind And Search Not To
Remember All That Has Hurt And Sent You
Spinning Out Of Control -
Do Not Try To Remember The Totally
Nebulous Conversation Between Conscious
And Sub Conscious, Reminding You That You
Are Out Of Control...Am I Resting Now? -- Closing
Doors To The Past -- Do I Fly Along
Or Have I Offered You Reality Instead?

Alive - Resting-Flow And Resisting, Desperate
Yet Together, Flying High, Yet Ground Bound --
Remind Me Why I Am Here?
Is There A Reason For My Existence?
Measuring The Moments, Alluring, Remote,
Resilient, Innovative -
Alive And Surviving Everyday Anew- Resolving
To Be, To Stay,
To Exist Beyond The Day...

Soul Reflections

Reviving The Bones Of Life - Dust And Ashes -
Heaven To Earth - Grave To Life -
A Constant Cycle Of Regeneration-

Black And White Hold On For Dear Life-
Color Does Not Matter In A Life And Death
Situation ... What A Pity Life And Death Does Not
Enter Into Interpersonal Relationships On
A Daily Basis-Prejudice Stinks...

I Am A Jewess - Wandering Mind And Spirit....
Ever, Never, For Ever -
Today Is Still Only Today...
Enter The Silver Skies Of Floating On Air Waves
Of Motion - Remind Me Of When I Was Flying With
You Amongst The Stratums -
I Am So Close To You - I Feel Your Nearness ...
Caught Adrift Between Reality And Illusion -
Separated By A Veil Of Clouds
In An Atmosphere Of Reverence And Calm.

Searching For A Meaning To My Existence
And Understanding That It Is "You"
Who Fulfills My Destiny ...

Existing But For The Thread Of Truth In A
Malignant And Static World -
Moving Through Dreams In A Blissful State
Of Ignorance-
Here But For The Grace Of Light
Do I Find My Way In The Darkness
Of A Road Traveled A Million Miles,
Yet Unknown!

Tiredness Befalls The Weary Traveler -
Sleep Eludes Him For The Road Is Hazardous And
Steep -
Sadness Follows Him ...
Yet Joy Seems Just Around The Bend,
Providing Sustenance And Focus -
A Road Of Long Awaited Bliss -
The Oasis Of Love Nourishing And Sustaining My
Soul!

I See You In My Minds Eye,
Hold You Fast, Afraid To Touch A Shadow
Or A Dream -

Soul Reflections

A Spirit, Or A Brilliant Facet Reflection Blue
White Diamonds, Glistening In The Sunshine
Of My Life -
Sacred Passage, Illuminate And Strengthen My
Resolve To Live Some More...

I Look At A Painting-
In My Mind I Am Thinking Of Your Response
To My Thoughts-
I Can Share My Feelings - You Don't Object.
Isn't It Grand To Be Able To Think Out Loud
And Not Be Chastised Or Laughed At -
Holding Hands - Energy Exchange-
So Much To Say And Always Full Of Love
And Gladness -
Would That It Be So Always -
I Feel, I See, I Elaborate And It's OK -
There Is Little Resistance To The View -
Just A Total Acceptance Of Who I Am-
Who We Are -
Falling In Love With The Idea
Of Being With Each Other -

Oh G-D Please Give Me Life To Experience
This-
To Live This-
To Accept This-
Let Me Rest My Weary Mind,
My Tormented Body,
My Aching Heart,
In The Arms Of My Beloved,
Who Revives In Me Eternal Gratitude
And Bliss Filling My Being With Joy
And.................

# Self Under Construction 1974/2002

A Process Ongoing

I Exist...But Who Am I?
A Shell Of A Person, Not Me At All -
Step Out Of Myself - Observe...
Perceive, Explore:
Open Eyes That Gaze, But Never See-
Pity!
Go Places That Were, But Never Truly Are-
Loss!
Experience Who I Thought Was Dead-
ME!

Who Is Me? Wretched, Wailing Body, Mutilated-
Mind Shattered, Bemoaning My Fate, Empty,
Tortured Soul, Miserable, Whimpering, Wailing,
Lamenting Losses Beyond Comprehension-
Is That Me?

Or Am I Ecstatic, Joyous, Spontaneous,
Delighting In The Mundane? Aware-
Alive-
Pulsating Energy, Life Force, Vibrant-
Relentlessly Striving For Future, Beyond Limitaton!
Powerfully Constructing Who I Want To BE!!!

Shell Of A Person??? Is That ME??

No! No More!
Emerge Woman! Lift Your Eyes!
Transform! Be!
Look At ME! Take Me In...
Now!!! World, NOW!!

# Voyage of the Soul

I Am Alone!
Surrounded By Circles Of Fire,
Smouldering Ambers;
Enveloping,
Permeating The Fiber Of Life,
In Midst Of Tears,
Shaken Beyond Recognition.

Wild Winds, Snowy Forests,
Black And Deep-
White Crested Waves,
Taller Than Mountains,
Thrown Onto Sparkling Sands,
Breathless, Torn, Fallen
Crazed And Beaten-
I Am Alive!

Destined, Chosen, Blessed
Raised, From Death,
Yet Once Again,
From Ashes:
Opening Doors To Life,
Beyond The Storms.

Slowly I Grow,
A Seed,
Frightened..
Weather And Wind,
Lest I Loose My Ground,
I Plant Roots,
Deep Bosom Of Earth Mother,
Wailing Bittersweet Tears
Of Memories And Remorse,
Trying To Comprehend -
Understand Less!

Safety Lies In The Essence Of Being,
In Choices That Travel Beyond Consciousness.
Knowledge Exists,
In A Piece Of Sky-
Saved For The Soul,
Once Again..

Soul Reflections

# The House

A House In The Valley,
Old Worn, Falling Apart...
Forgotten -
Left Long Ago To Wind, Storm And Sun -
Overgrown:
Green Locks Of Ivy Frolicking,
Falling, Curling, 'Round Every Nook 'N Cranny
Holding On To History And Past,
Memories Left Behind,
Laughter And Joy. Youth Unbound...
Bricks And Mortar, Cementing The Years.

Once I Lived Here,
The House Glimmering In Its Glory
Welcoming, Inviting, Beckoning...
So Much Love In Those Days - Fun And Laughter
Racing Through Fields.... Careless, Free,
Days Of Never Ending Summers-
Frosty, Snow Laden Winters,
Friends, Young Lovers, Tears...
The House Heard, Saw, Lived, Breathed
Steadfast, Providing, Sheltering, Protecting....

Then One Day We Left,
Took Our Dreams To The City,
Trading Trees, Birds And Flowers
For Tall Buildings, Money And Noise
Rarely Reminiscing Days Gone By,
Barely Mentioning The House....

Years Have Passed, Life Itself....
Lately My Dreams Return To Soft Grass,
Wildflowers, Bees Buzzing, Familiar, Forgotten Smells
Thoughts Hovering Above My Childhood,
Reliving My Fondest Moments:
A Lifetime Passed Too Soon,
Taken For Granted, Time Conceded,
Autumn, Winter- Seasons Gone....
On My Way To Eternal Spring,
Shedding A Tear....
Remembering And Blessing The House....

*Dedicated To My Dear Beloved Friend And Student Angela Benne*

<u>Soul Reflections</u>

Snake Woman

Pastel On Paper

_Soul Reflections_